Black Men IN SCIENCE

15 INSPIRING PEOPLE YOU SHOULD KNOW

A BLACK HISTORY BOOK FOR KIDS

Bryan Patrick Avery

Illustrations by by Nikita Leanne

ROCKRIDGE PRESS

For general information on our other products and services or to obtain technical support, please contact our Customer Care Department within the United States at (866) 744-2665, or outside the United States at (510) 253-0500.

Rockridge Press publishes its books in a variety of electronic and print formats. Some content that appears in print may not be available in electronic books, and vice versa.

Series Designer: Will Mack
Interior and Cover Designer: Linda Kocur
Art Producer: Melissa Malinowksy
Editor: Eliza Kirby
Production Editor: Jael Fogle
Production Manager: Jose Olivera

Paperback ISBN: 978-1-63878-215-5
eBook ISBN: 978-1-63878-288-9
R0

Printed in China

Black Men in Science

For Ashley.
May your own dreams be your only boundaries.

Contents

Introduction

Throughout history, scientists have asked questions and searched for answers. Many of these answers have transformed our lives. By hypothesizing and experimenting their way to discoveries, scientists have shaped the world around us. Many of them, like Thomas Edison and Nikola Tesla, are well known. Many Black scientists who have made groundbreaking contributions to their fields are not.

This book highlights the accomplishments of 15 Black men in science and technology. Despite racism and inequality, these men persevered and succeeded. They excelled in their fields. They challenged the belief that Black people were less capable than white people.

Edward Bouchet was the first Black man to earn a PhD from an American university. No college would hire him as a professor, but he inspired generations of students to pursue science. Fighter pilot and engineer Guion Bluford Jr. became the first African American in space.

He paved the way for countless men and women of color to enter space exploration. These are just a couple of the trailblazers and changemakers you will meet in this book. As you read their stories, you'll find resources and interactive features that let you explore more. When you see a tricky word in **bold**, flip to the glossary at the back of the book to learn its definition.

The people in this book are only a few of the Black men who contributed to the sciences. Hopefully, their stories will spark your curiosity and inspire you. There's much still to discover in our world and beyond. Will you follow in their footsteps and make the next great discovery?

James McCune SMITH

1813–1865

In the 1830s, it was difficult for a Black man to get into an American university. That didn't stop James McCune Smith from seeking an education. He traveled all the way to Scotland and attended Glasgow University. James became the first African American to earn a medical degree. Returning home, he put his knowledge to work. As a doctor, he helped heal the sick. As an **abolitionist**, he worked to rid the country of slavery.

James was born on April 18, 1813, in New York. His mother, Lavinia Smith, was enslaved. She purchased her own freedom by paying the man who enslaved her to let her go free. It is not clear who James's father was. Many believe it was Lavinia's former enslaver, a merchant named Samuel Smith.

James grew up in New York and attended New York City's African Free School #2. Among his fellow students were Ira Aldridge, Henry Garnet, and Charles Reason. Ira became a leading Shakespearean actor. Henry's work as a minister gave him a platform to fight for an end to slavery. Charles Reason grew up to become a professor.

James graduated from the Free School with honors and was eager to continue his education. He worked with tutors to learn Greek and Latin and applied to universities in hopes of getting a medical degree. But his applications were rejected because he was Black. Undeterred, James applied to Glasgow University in Scotland. Glasgow had no restrictions on students based on the color of their skin. James was admitted in 1832 and began his studies.

Glasgow was a center of the abolitionist movement in the United Kingdom. James became a cofounder of the Glasgow **Emancipation** Society just before Britain outlawed slavery in 1833. All the while, he continued his academic success at Glasgow University. James earned his bachelor's, master's, and medical degrees in just five years. Normally, earning all three degrees would take at least 10 years. After completing his **residency** in Paris, James chose to return home to America.

Once back in New York, James opened a medical practice and a pharmacy. It was the first Black-owned pharmacy in the United States. James served patients regardless of color. Many considered him to be one of the best doctors in New York.

In 1840, James wrote the first medical case study by a Black doctor. He was not allowed to present the paper to the New York Medical and Surgical Society. The society was concerned that presenting a Black man's work would create a problem for its membership. But a short time later, James wrote a paper on the effects of the drug opium, which was published in a medical journal.

James also became the medical director of the Colored Orphan Asylum. It was a place where Black children whose parents had died or could not care for them received shelter and schooling. The asylum had a high death rate. The previous director blamed this on the fact that the patients were Black. James objected to this conclusion. As director, he slowed the spread of diseases by implementing social distancing between patients.

Besides practicing medicine, James worked with other abolitionists to bring about racial equality. He used science and **statistics** to disprove a government report that said Black people who were enslaved were happier and healthier than free Black people. This false claim was based on data from the 1840 **census**. James showed that the data was inaccurate. In one example, James showed that the census counted more mentally ill Black people than the total number of Black citizens. Because of James's work, many who supported the report's original findings changed their minds.

In 1855, James helped found the Radical Political Abolitionists. They advocated for an end to slavery and support of formerly enslaved people. Frederick Douglass and Gerrit Smith were also cofounders.

James's work as a physician left an enduring mark on America. His skill as a physician proved that Black people could excel in that field. His work as an abolitionist was equally important. By challenging claims of African inferiority, James helped some Americans begin to see Black people and white people as equals. His journey, from New York to Glasgow and back again, is a story of determination and perseverance. He found a way to get a medical degree when it looked like every door was closed. He kept writing, even when he couldn't get published. Most of all, he stood up for others to ensure that even if he was the first, he would not be the last.

EXPLORE MORE! To learn more about James, visit the James McCune Smith pavilion in the DiMenna Children's History Museum in New York City. You can find out about the pavilion through the New-York Historical Society at NYHistory.org/childrens-museum.

DID YOU KNOW? As a young student at New York African Free School #2, James was invited to speak during the visit of the Marquis de Lafayette, a Revolutionary War hero.

Lewis Howard LATIMER

1848–1928

Inventors rarely work alone. Most **collaborate** with others to perfect their ideas and document their creations. In the late 1800s, America's most renowned inventors turned to Lewis Howard Latimer. Lewis worked with Hiram Maxim and Thomas Edison on the breakthrough invention of **incandescent** lighting. He also worked with Alexander Graham Bell on the **patent** application for the telephone. With Lewis's expertise and assistance, these inventors and their inventions revolutionized the world.

Lewis was born on September 4, 1848, in Massachusetts. His parents, George and Rebecca Latimer, had escaped from slavery several years earlier. They fled Virginia and went north in search of freedom. In grammar school, Lewis showed great promise. He was a good student who enjoyed reading and drawing. In 1857, when Lewis was nine years old, his father disappeared. Lewis's mother did all she could to take care of her four children, but it was difficult.

In 1864, with the Civil War raging, Lewis lied about his age to enlist in the United States Navy. He was just 16 years old. When the war ended a year later, Lewis returned home to Boston to look for a job.

In 1868, the law firm Crosby and Gould hired Lewis as an office boy. The company worked on patent law, which helps inventors protect their **intellectual property**. A patent ensures other people must pay to use a creator's intellectual property.

Crosby and Gould employed drafters to draw designs of inventions for patent applications. Technical drawing, or drafting, is very difficult. It requires the drafter to create detailed drawings without making mistakes. Lewis read books and watched the drafters in the office to teach himself technical drawing. He learned to use T squares, compasses, and other drawing aids.

After several months of studying and practice, Lewis asked his firm for the opportunity to demonstrate his skill. They agreed. He was so impressive that he was promoted from office boy to drafter. His salary increased from $3 a week to $20 a week. Most importantly, Lewis's new job opened a whole new world of opportunity. While working for Crosby and Gould, Lewis was approached by Alexander Graham Bell. He needed help applying for a patent for his latest invention: the telephone. Bell was racing against another inventor, Elisha Gray, to patent the telephone. He needed help to win the race.

Working at night with Bell, Lewis created the technical drawings of the telephone. He also provided guidance based on his knowledge of the application process. On February 14, 1876, Bell's patent application was submitted. Bell received the patent, and his rival missed out.

In 1880, Lewis went to work for the United States Electric Lighting Company as a drafter. The company was founded by inventor Hiram Maxim and focused on electric lighting. Electric lighting was very competitive, and inventors scrambled to secure patents to protect their work. Lewis had the opportunity to learn all about the field. He even traveled around the world, supervising the production and installation of the company's equipment in Canada and England.

Lewis's talents did not go unnoticed. In 1884, he was recruited to work for Thomas Edison, Maxim's biggest rival. Lewis's **engineering** knowledge, as well as his deep understanding of the electric light, made him a valuable resource for Edison.

In 1890, at Edison's urging, Lewis wrote a book explaining how the electric light worked. The book was called *Incandescent Electric Lighting: A Practical Description of the Edison System*. It was written in simple, easy-to-read language and helped everyday people understand and accept electric lighting. This was important because people at the time used candles and oil lamps for light. Electricity was new, and many were worried it was unsafe.

Lewis advised Edison on his patents, ensuring they were submitted correctly so that Edison's interests would be protected. He also became Edison's patent investigator.

He was responsible for ensuring other companies weren't making money from Edison's patents without Edison's permission. He even acted as an expert witness in cases where he believed Edison's patents had been used improperly.

In addition to helping other inventors, Lewis obtained several patents of his own. One was an improvement to Edison's design for the lightbulb. Another was for a toilet in railroad cars, something that didn't exist at the time. Lewis even received a patent for an early air conditioner. He remained a patent consultant until 1922, when he had to retire due to his failing eyesight.

Lewis's talent and determination led him to partner with some of history's most important inventors. Who knows what would have happened if Bell's application for the telephone patent had not been submitted when it was. Without Lewis's book on how the lightbulb works, would Edison's invention have taken the world by storm? We simply don't know. What we do know is that Lewis played an important role in two inventions that changed the world. Though his name may not be as well known as others, his contributions are no less important. No one can succeed alone. Lewis was the ultimate partner.

"WE CREATE OUR FUTURE BY WELL IMPROVING PRESENT OPPORTUNITIES, HOWEVER FEW AND SMALL THEY BE."

EXPLORE MORE! Learn more about electricity and how it powers our world with a virtual tour of the Spark Museum of Electrical Invention at SparkMuseum.org/virtual-visit.

DID YOU KNOW? Lewis was one of the Edison Pioneers, a group of people who worked closely with Thomas Edison prior to 1885. He was the only Black member of the group.

F=ma
P=E/t
W=Fs
W=mg
v=d/t
a=Dv/t

Edward Alexander BOUCHET

1852–1918

As a young boy, Edward Bouchet's educational options were limited. Despite this, Edward worked his way into Yale College and was elected to the honor society Phi Beta Kappa. He then earned a doctorate in **physics**, becoming the first African American to earn a PhD in America. Edward's passion for learning served as an inspiration to all those he taught. His impact on people seeking higher education even continues today.

Edward was born in New Haven, Connecticut, on September 15, 1852. He was the youngest of four children. His father, William, a formerly enslaved person, worked as a **porter** at Yale College. Edward's mother, Susan, also worked at Yale, washing the students' laundry.

There weren't many schools available to Edward in New Haven. At the time, the schools were **segregated**, and only a few admitted Black students. Edward attended the Artisan Street Colored School. It was a one-room schoolhouse with one teacher and 30 students across many grades. He excelled in his studies there and at New Haven High School.

In 1868, he was accepted into Hopkins Grammar School. Hopkins was a **prestigious** private school in New Haven that prepared its students to attend Yale College. Edward graduated at the top of his class. In the fall of 1870 he entered Yale, where he continued to excel. He took a wide variety of courses, including languages like German, Latin, and Greek. He also studied math, astronomy, and physics.

Edward graduated from Yale in 1874, sixth in his class of 124 students. In recognition of his academic achievement, he was elected to Phi Beta Kappa. He was the first Black student nominated for such an honor.

Edward's skill in the sciences caught the eye of Alfred Cope. Cope was a **philanthropist** with an interest in civil rights. He was on the board of directors for the Institute for Colored Youth (ICY). ICY was an all-Black high school in Philadelphia, Pennsylvania. Cope hoped to convince Edward to teach at ICY. Cope knew, however, that Edward needed to continue his education first. Edward went on to postgraduate studies at Yale, studying physics under Arthur Wright. Wright was the first person to earn a doctorate in physics from an American university.

Cope continued to help Edward, giving him money and encouragement. Edward focused his attention on a branch of physics called geometrical optics. Just two years after receiving his undergraduate degree, Edward earned his PhD. He was the first African American to earn a PhD from an American university.

Despite his achievements, racial injustice prevented Edward from reaping the benefits of his hard work. He searched for a job as a professor but was unable to find one at an American university. In 1876, he accepted Alfred Cope's invitation to teach at ICY.

Edward led the school's new science program. He taught many science courses, including physics, geography, and astronomy. In addition to his regular classes, Edward gave lectures to the teachers on science topics. He even hosted lectures for the local community. Edward believed in improving science education, so he went to the board of the school and advocated for them to spend money on better laboratory facilities. This, he believed, would aid the students' learning and development.

For 26 years, Edward taught at ICY. Then the school's focus began to change. In the early 1900s, many educators believed that Black students were best suited for vocational training. Vocational training teaches students skills needed for a specific job, like nursing or construction. It was argued that Black students did not have the skills for academic pursuits. Even Booker T. Washington, founder of Tuskegee Institute, was in favor of this. Edward's success in the sciences was a clear argument against this theory.

Even so, in 1902, ICY abandoned its academic departments to focus on providing vocational training. Edward lost his job. For the next 14 years, Edward traveled the country working at various schools in Missouri and Virginia. In 1908, he became the principal of Lincoln High

School in Gallipolis, Ohio. He served as principal there until 1913.

When he died in 1918, Edward left little behind. Unlike many scientists, he left no notes or journals. We don't know much about how he felt regarding his challenges or successes. What he did leave behind was the proof that anyone, regardless of the color of their skin, is capable of success. Edward's achievements debunked the myth that Black people couldn't succeed in the academic world. His lectures inspired others to follow in his footsteps and study the sciences. From the tombstone erected in his honor at Yale to an academic honor society named after him, Edward remains an inspiration to scientists more than 100 years after his death.

EXPLORE MORE! Edward's field of study was physics, the science of matter, energy, and force. Learn more about physics in Neil deGrasse Tyson's book *Astrophysics for Young People in a Hurry*, written with Gregory Mone.

DID YOU KNOW? The Edward Alexander Bouchet Graduate Honor Society was founded in 2005. With nearly 20 chapters around the country, its goal is to honor and continue Edward Bouchet's contributions to those seeking higher education.

George Washington CARVER

1864–1943

George Washington Carver was born into slavery. This experience inspired him to help the poorest farmers in the South. George taught farmers to rotate the crops they planted, which renewed the soil that had been hurt by years of cotton growing. When crop rotation led to a crop **surplus**, George invented hundreds of products using sweet potatoes and peanuts. Many of those products are still used today. Known as the Peanut Man, George was one of America's greatest inventors, scientists, and educators.

George was born on a farm in Diamond Grove, Missouri, in 1864. His mother was an enslaved person working on the farm. His father died in an accident before George was born. The farm was owned by Moses and Susan Carver. Not long after George was born, slave raiders kidnapped George, his mother, and his sister. The raiders hoped to sell them in Kentucky. Moses paid his neighbor to reclaim George and his family. The neighbor was only able to find George. He traded one of the Carvers' best horses in exchange for George.

Slavery was abolished in the United States in 1865, when George was a baby. Moses and Susan raised George. They even taught him to read and write, which was rare at that time. When he grew old enough to work in the fields, George was too sickly to do so. Instead, Susan taught him to cook, sew, and garden. George even learned how to make herbal medicines. Even though he was young, George showed a keen interest in plants and plant **biology**. Farmers in the area came to him for help because he was so good at diagnosing problems in their fields and orchards.

When he was 11, George moved to the town of Neosho, not far from the farm. There, he attended an all-Black elementary school. He lived with Andrew and Mariah Watkins, who had no children of their own. They offered George free room and board. All he had to do was help with chores around the house. George continued learning about medicinal herbs from Mariah.

At that time, many African Americans were moving west in search of opportunities. George joined the migration. He ended up in Kansas, where he graduated from Minneapolis High School in 1880. After high school, George applied to Highland College in Kansas and was accepted. Highland was an all-white school. When George arrived for classes and the school saw he was Black, he was not allowed to attend.

George moved to Iowa and, in 1890, enrolled in Simpson College. Before long, one of his professors noticed George's interest in **botany**. He encouraged George to transfer to the Iowa State Agricultural School, where he could study plants. George took his advice and, in 1894, became the first African American to earn a Bachelor of Science degree. Two years later, George earned his Master of Agriculture degree. He had become well known for his work with plants during his time in Iowa, so it was no surprise that many schools wanted him to work at their campuses. George chose to work at Tuskegee Institute, a historically Black college in Alabama.

George was intent on making sure his work helped Black farmers. Being at Tuskegee gave him the chance to do just that. George researched and taught at the Institute. He also spent time working with local farmers and helping them run productive farms.

Cotton was the main crop at that time. Farmers noticed that cotton was not growing as well as it had in the past. George explained that growing cotton year after year in the same place had hurt the soil. He taught the farmers that the solution was to rotate the crops they planted. By planting different crops, like peanuts and sweet potatoes, the farmers refreshed the soil. Then things like cotton would grow more easily. The farmers took George's advice and started rotating crops. It solved the cotton problem, but it also presented a new challenge. What could they do with all these peanuts and sweet potatoes?

George went back to his lab and found a solution. Actually, more than 300 solutions! Using his creativity, George invented hundreds of uses for sweet potatoes and peanuts. He showed how vinegar, milk, flour, and cooking oil could be made from the crops. He even invented ways to turn the crops into soap, paper, cosmetics, and ink.

In 1921, George spoke to Congress in favor of a **tariff** on imported peanuts. The tariff would make peanuts brought from overseas more expensive, which would protect the American peanut market. George received a standing ovation at the end of his speech. Congress passed the tariff. The United States of America is now the fourth largest peanut producer in the world.

George's contribution to history goes beyond science, education, or farming. His life's work to uplift struggling farmers shows a humanitarian side that isn't often remembered. Many times, scientists and inventors experiment for the sake of gaining knowledge. George used the knowledge he gained from his experiments to change the world. That is his legacy.

"IT IS NOT THE STYLE OF CLOTHES ONE WEARS, NEITHER THE KIND OF AUTOMOBILE ONE DRIVES, NOR THE AMOUNT OF MONEY ONE HAS IN THE BANK, THAT COUNTS. THESE MEAN NOTHING. IT IS SIMPLY SERVICE THAT MEASURES SUCCESS."

EXPLORE MORE! Want to learn about George Washington Carver and his work? Visit the National Park Service's George Washington Carver online exhibit at NPS.gov/museum/exhibits/tuskegee/gwcarver.

DID YOU KNOW? George's childhood home in Diamond, Missouri, was designated a national monument in 1943. It was the first time a national monument had been created for someone other than a president.

Charles Henry TURNER

1867–1923

Scientists have long been fascinated by animal behavior. Why do bears rub up against trees after hibernating? How do bees find their hives? Why do dogs turn in a circle before lying down? Charles Henry Turner was a pioneer in the study of animal behavior. He wrote more than 70 scientific papers on the subject during his 33-year career. His success is particularly impressive because he worked without the resources that other researchers had. Still, Charles managed to become a leader in his field.

Charles was born on February 3, 1867, in Cincinnati, Ohio, to Thomas and Addie Turner. His father worked at a local church as a custodian. His mother was a nurse. His parents, freed from slavery during the Civil War, encouraged Charles to get a good education.

Charles was **valedictorian** of his graduating class at Gaines High School in 1886 and entered the University of Cincinnati. At Cincinnati, he majored in biology, the study of living things, and earned a Bachelor of Science degree in 1891. A year later, Charles earned his Master of Science degree, also from the University of Cincinnati.

In search of a teaching position, Charles moved to Atlanta, Georgia, and became the chair of the science department at Clark College, a historically Black college. Charles taught at Clark for 12 years before leaving to continue his studies at the University of Chicago. In 1907, Charles earned his doctorate in **zoology**. He was the first African American to earn a doctorate degree from the University of Chicago. For his doctorate, Charles studied how ants locate their nests. He noted that they make a circling motion when they return to their nests. This movement is now known as Turner circling.

After receiving his doctorate degree, Charles was unable to get a teaching position at the University of Chicago. He moved to St. Louis, Missouri, where he took a job at Sumner High School. It was the first high school for African American students west of the Mississippi River.

In addition to teaching, Charles continued his scientific research. He lacked the resources and laboratory space of his peers at universities. Nevertheless, he published an average of two papers per year. That was more than most of his fellow scientists.

Charles worked with many different animals, including bees, ants, pigeons, crustaceans, and spiders. This required learning different ways to raise and care for the animals. It also required different methods for studying them. Without a formal lab space, Charles had to perform his experiments during his free time. This meant doing research in the evenings or during summer when school was not in session.

Charles designed several different tools to help in his experiments. He built mazes for cockroaches and colored boxes to test the vision of honeybees. Many of Charles's experiments focused on the behavior of animals. He studied how insects navigate and learn, and even how some pretend to be dead to avoid predators.

At the time, it was widely believed that insects could not learn new behaviors. Charles conducted a maze experiment with cockroaches that challenged this belief. He saw that when a cockroach learned to avoid a dark chamber in one maze, it would avoid dark chambers in other mazes as well. His observations proved that insects could change their behavior based on their experience. They could learn!

Charles used bees in his research, but he also used them as teaching aids for his students. At Sumner High School, he conducted an experiment in which he placed a jar of jam on the table at each meal. Bees would come to the table at breakfast, lunch, and dinner. When he stopped putting the jam out at lunch and dinner, the bees eventually stopped coming to those meals. Through this experiment, Charles demonstrated that bees had some concept of time.

Charles's work changed how we understand animal behavior. Many of his discoveries helped spark additional discoveries by later scientists. Born just two years after the end of the Civil War, Charles faced racism and prejudice for his entire professional career. It impacted the jobs he was able to get and the pay he received. That did not stop him in his quest to gain and share knowledge. On the contrary, it inspired him to encourage others to follow in his footsteps.

Charles became an advocate for civil rights, believing that education was the way to end racism and inequality. As a result, Charles often took lower-paying jobs at predominantly Black schools so he could pass his wisdom along and help develop the next generation of Black students. In recognition of Charles's educational and scientific contributions, a number of schools across the United States have been named in his honor.

EXPLORE MORE! To learn more about Charles's work and to try your hand at bug watching, check out *Bug Watching with Charles Henry Turner* by Michael Elsohn Ross and Laurie A. Caple.

DID YOU KNOW? Charles attempted to get a teaching position at Tuskegee Institute, but the school couldn't afford to pay both him and fellow Black scientist George Washington Carver.

Percy Lavon JULIAN

1899–1975

Chemistry is the study of substances and how they behave. In the early 20th century, chemists were in high demand. Percy Lavon Julian overcame racism and segregation to become one of America's leading chemists. He developed **synthetic** hormones and used them to fight various diseases. Percy's work helped ease the pain of many sick people.

Percy was born on April 11, 1899, in Montgomery, Alabama. He was the grandson of formerly enslaved people. Both of his parents were educated. Percy's father, James, was a railroad mail clerk. His mother, Elizabeth, was a schoolteacher. Percy's parents believed in the value of an education.

The schools in Montgomery were segregated, so Percy attended a Black elementary school. There were no Black high schools in Montgomery, so Percy attended the State Normal School for Negroes. The Normal School was a teacher-training school. He didn't plan to become a teacher, but it was the only place he could continue his education.

In 1916, Percy applied to DePauw University. Located in Indiana, DePauw accepted Black and white students. Because he had not attended high school, Percy began as a **probationary** student. This meant he had to take high school classes along with his college courses. Percy worked hard and was named a member of the Sigma Xi honor society. He was also elected to Phi Beta Kappa. In 1920, Percy graduated at the top of his class with a degree in chemistry.

Despite his success at DePauw, Percy's professors discouraged him from continuing his studies. Instead, he took a position teaching chemistry at Fisk University. Fisk was a Black college in Tennessee. While at Fisk, Percy was awarded the Austin Fellowship in Chemistry. The fellowship paid Percy's costs to pursue a graduate degree at Harvard University. He moved to Massachusetts and received his master's degree in chemistry in 1923. He got an A in every course he took and graduated first in his class.

Even though Percy had proven himself at Harvard, the school refused to admit him to its doctoral program. Harvard would not allow Percy to be a teaching assistant. They were concerned that white students would not accept a Black teacher. Being a teaching assistant was a requirement for the doctoral program, so Percy couldn't continue his studies there.

Percy went to teach at West Virginia State College for Negroes. Then he moved to Howard University. Both schools served Black students, so Percy was allowed to work there. But he still wanted to earn his doctorate degree. In 1929, he received a fellowship to continue his studies. Percy moved to Austria to attend the University of Vienna. In Austria, Percy discovered that the color of his skin wasn't as much of a problem as it was in the United States. He still faced some discrimination, but he began to experience freedom in new ways.

Percy studied organic chemistry at the University of Vienna. As he studied, he developed an interest in the soybean. This interest would guide his career and lead to some of Percy's biggest discoveries.

In 1931, after earning his PhD, Percy returned to the United States. He went back to Howard University for two years. Then he accepted a research position at DePauw University, his **alma mater**. At DePauw, Percy became an expert in synthesis. Synthesis uses a series of chemical reactions to turn one substance into another. In 1935, Percy and his colleague Josef Pikl used synthesis to produce a chemical called physostigmine.

Physostigmine is used to treat glaucoma, an eye disease that can cause blindness. The chemical comes from the Calabar bean. Natural physostigmine is very expensive because it is difficult to extract from the bean. The synthetic version was much cheaper to produce. That meant more patients suffering from disease could afford treatment.

A year later, Percy wrote to the Glidden Company. The company made paints and varnishes as well as dog food, candies, and cosmetics. His intent was to ask them for information on soybeans. Instead, Glidden offered Percy a job. He joined their soybean division as director of research in 1936.

At Glidden, Percy developed new methods for mass-producing different hormones. Many medicines used hormones, and Percy's work ensured that these medicines were available whenever people needed them. Percy's method for synthesizing hydrocortisone, which is used to help with rashes and other itchy conditions, is still used today.

In 1953, Percy started his own company, Julian Laboratories. His goal was to continue his work synthesizing hormones. Percy recruited many of the top chemists at Glidden to his new company. He also began hiring young Black chemists so that he could mentor them. He sold his company in 1961 for $2 million. Today, that would be equal to more than $18 million!

Despite the obstacles placed in front of him, Percy was determined to succeed. He never stopped working toward his goal of earning a doctorate degree. Though his quest took him all the way to Europe, Percy returned to the United States. He wanted to make a difference in his own country. Percy worked tirelessly to improve the world, both scientifically and socially. His work in the lab, which led to more than 100 patents, eased the suffering of the sick. His work mentoring scientists ensured more Black scientists would follow in his path. Percy's work as a chemist, businessman, and leader made a difference.

"I HAVE HAD ONE GOAL IN MY LIFE, THAT OF PLAYING SOME ROLE IN MAKING LIFE A LITTLE EASIER FOR THE PERSONS WHO COME AFTER ME."

EXPLORE MORE! Want to try out a few experiments of your own? Check out *Real Chemistry Experiments: 40 Exciting STEAM Activities for Kids* by Edward P. Zovinka, PhD.

DID YOU KNOW? In 1947, Percy received the Spingarn Medal from the National Association for the Advancement of Colored People (NAACP). The NAACP wanted to recognize his "many important discoveries that have saved many lives."

Leonidas Harris BERRY

1902–1995

Leonidas Berry called himself a multidimensional doctor. Why? Because he was a physician, inventor, and teacher. He was also an author and an activist. Leonidas invented a tool that allowed doctors to safely study patients' stomachs without needing to do surgery. He wrote almost 100 articles for medical journals. He fought to end discrimination in the medical field. He also paved the way for more doctors of color to follow in his footsteps.

Leonidas was born on July 20, 1902, in North Carolina. His mother, Beulah, was a schoolteacher. His father, Llewellyn, was a minister in the African Methodist Episcopal Church (AME Church). Leonidas grew up in Norfolk, where he attended high school.

After high school, Leonidas attended Wilberforce University in Ohio. Wilberforce was run by the AME Church. It was the first college owned and run by African Americans. Leonidas earned his Bachelor of Science degree in 1924. A year later, he earned another degree from the University of Chicago. Then he enrolled in its medical school. In 1929, Leonidas graduated from Rush Medical College at the University of Chicago. He continued his studies, earning a Master of Science degree in **pathology**, the study of diseases, in 1933.

His formal education complete, Leonidas went to work at Provident Hospital. Provident was a Black hospital in Chicago. He chose to specialize in gastroenterology, the study of the digestive system. Around this time, an improved version of an instrument called a gastroscope hit the market. Gastroscopes allow doctors to view a patient's digestive system. Older scopes were rigid, but this gastroscope used a flexible tube. The new design made it easier to use. It also made it safer for the patient. Leonidas was fascinated by this new tool and wanted to learn more about it.

Rudolf Schindler had designed the new scope. He had recently arrived in America from Germany and joined the faculty at the University of Chicago. Leonidas asked his mentor for an introduction to Rudolf. For a year, Leonidas studied under Rudolf, learning how to use the gastroscope.

In 1937, Leonidas started a gastroscopy clinic at Provident Hospital. He bought a Schindler-designed gastroscope to use in the clinic. Leonidas quickly became a recognized expert in the field. He performed more than 5,000 procedures in his career. In addition to treating patients, Leonidas used the device to study the stomachs of alcoholics. At that time, doctors believed alcohol damaged the stomach. In his research, Leonidas discovered that drinking too much alcohol actually damaged the liver. Leonidas presented his results at an American Medical Association (AMA) convention in 1941. He was the first African American to present to the AMA. His discovery changed how doctors treated the health problems associated with alcoholism.

In 1955, Leonidas invented an attachment for the gastroscope. It was called the Eder-Berry biopsy attachment. This instrument allowed doctors to remove sick **tissue** samples that they could examine. That meant doctors could take samples without performing surgery, which was much safer for the patient.

Besides his duties at various hospitals around Chicago, Leonidas volunteered in the community. He became president of the Cook County Physicians Association (CCPA) in 1950. The group addressed problems in medicine caused by race and economic status. As president of CCPA, Leonidas created a drug **rehabilitation** program. The program got the attention of Illinois governor Adlai Stevenson. The governor created an advisory committee on treating addiction and asked Leonidas to join. Leonidas recommended creating four clinics around Cook County. Three would be in hospitals, and the fourth would be in the county jail. Each clinic would focus on the medical needs of patients struggling with addiction. Before, addicts were simply treated like criminals. The state of

Illinois approved Leonidas's plan. It came to be known as the Berry Plan. The plan operated from 1951 to 1958 and helped countless addicts.

Although Leonidas was a successful and well-respected doctor, he still experienced racism throughout his career. This inspired him to work to end discrimination in the medical field. In 1964, the Civil Rights Act became law. Medicare was created a year later. Both laws had anti-segregation rules that prevented doctors and hospitals from denying care to Black people. Leonidas fought to make sure that hospitals obeyed these new laws. He was elected president of the National Medical Association (NMA) in 1965. The NMA is an organization of Black doctors. Leonidas used his platform to pressure the American Medical Association to end its practice of excluding Black doctors from its membership. In 1968, the AMA ended its approval of all-white chapters.

Leonidas's work to help the underserved extended beyond Cook County. When he heard that Black people struggled to get medical care in Cairo, Illinois, he wanted to help. Cairo was nearly 400 miles from Chicago. Leonidas gathered a group of doctors, technicians, and nurses. He **chartered** a plane to fly from Chicago to Cairo to provide medical services to those in need. The group became known as the Flying Black Medics.

Throughout his career, Leonidas found a way to make positive change in the world. His invention of the Eder-Berry attachment changed how doctors examined patients. His work on addiction revolutionized medical treatment for addicts. His efforts to fight discrimination gave hope to underserved communities. Leonidas truly was a multidimensional doctor.

EXPLORE MORE! Want to learn more about the human body and how it works? Check out *Human Anatomy Activity Book for Kids* by Shannan Muskopf, MS.

DID YOU KNOW? In 1921, while at Wilberforce University, Leonidas joined Alpha Phi Alpha Fraternity, Inc. This fraternity includes Dr. Martin Luther King Jr., Thurgood Marshall, and Garrett Morgan among its members.

Harold AMOS

1918–2003

Harold Amos was many things: Doctor. Researcher. Teacher. Pianist. He was a leader in the fields of **microbiology** and genetics. He was the first Black department head at Harvard Medical School. He also made time to mentor underrepresented students studying for careers in science.

Harold was born in 1918 in Pennsauken, New Jersey. His father, Howard, worked for the post office. His mother, Iola, worked as a maid in the home of a prominent Quaker family in Philadelphia. The family had raised Iola and homeschooled her with their own children. When she was an adult, the family gave Iola books to share with her own family. One of Harold's favorite books was a biography of scientist Louis Pasteur. This book sparked a love of science in Harold that stayed with him for the rest of his life.

Like most Black children at the time, Harold attended a segregated elementary school. Later, he graduated from Camden High School at the top of his class.

In 1936, he received a full academic scholarship to Springfield College. Black students were rarely offered such scholarships.

Harold majored in biology and minored in chemistry. In 1941, he graduated with honors. He began work as a graduate assistant in the college's biology department the next year. Then World War II began.

In December 1941, the United States entered World War II. The government began to draft young men to serve in the war. In 1942, Harold was drafted into the United States Army. He left his job at Springfield College and joined the army's Quartermaster Corps.

Harold served for two years in England before being transferred to France. While he was there, he fell in love with French culture. His admiration continued after he was released from the army in 1946. Harold even kept in touch with the French families who had welcomed him into their homes during the war.

When Harold returned to the United States, he enrolled at Harvard Medical School. A year later, he earned a Master of Arts degree. Then, in 1952, he earned his PhD. Harold was the first African American to earn a doctorate from the school. After being awarded a Fulbright fellowship, a special grant that allows students to study in other countries, he returned to France. There, he studied bacteria at the Pasteur Institute, a research organization named in honor of his childhood hero.

In 1954, Harold returned to Harvard Medical School and joined the faculty. He continued his research on bacteria, but his main focus over the rest of his career was animal cells. Harold became chair of the microbiology and molecular genetics department. He was the first African American department chair at Harvard Medical School. He served from 1968 to 1971 and then again from 1975 to 1978. He was also chair of the division of medical sciences from 1971 to 1975 and from 1978 until he retired in 1988.

These positions allowed Harold to shape the future of the school. They also gave him a way to help others follow in his footsteps. Harold tried to encourage students of color to pursue careers in science and medicine. In the 1980s, he supported the Hinton-Wright Society at Harvard. The society helped underrepresented students at Harvard's medical and dental schools.

Harold also served as director of the Minority Medical Faculty Development Program (MMFDP). The goal of the program was to increase the number of medical school faculty from underrepresented backgrounds. Since 1983, the program has produced 103 professors and 143 associate and assistant professors. Eight alumni of the program are deans or presidents of medical schools or colleges. After Harold's death, the MMFDP was renamed in his honor. It is now called the Harold Amos Medical Faculty Development Program.

Even after leaving Harvard, Harold continued to recruit students into science careers at Springfield College and Harvard. He also continued to serve on the board at Springfield for many years.

Harold's career spanned segregation, a world war, the civil rights movement, and beyond. He never stopped working to contribute to science and society. In the lab, his discoveries helped us understand how bacteria grow and mutate. Outside the lab, he brought generations of underrepresented students into the sciences. He laid the groundwork for organizations to continue recruiting and developing the talent of new scientists. Harold was a leader in his field, but he never let his success go to his head. After his death, Harold's Harvard peers praised his "selfless dedication to the personal as well as scientific welfare of their associates and students." Perhaps Harold's greatest achievement was that he left the world a little better than he found it.

EXPLORE MORE! To learn more about bacteria and viruses, check out *It's Catching: The Infectious World of Germs and Microbes* by Jennifer Gardy, PhD.

DID YOU KNOW? Harold was an excellent pianist with a passion for classical music. During his second trip to France, he spent time with many talented jazz musicians, including Ella Fitzgerald and Louis Armstrong.

David Harold BLACKWELL

1919–2010

David Harold Blackwell had a talent for seeing things no one had noticed before. This led him to incredible discoveries. During his long career, David worked in many different areas. He invented dynamic programming, a mathematical method that is still used today in finance and science. He also created the Rao-Blackwell theorem, which became one of the fundamental concepts in statistics. His simplified approach to teaching made David an excellent teacher and mentor. His passion for the "beauty" of mathematics was evident in his accomplishments.

David was born on April 24, 1919, in Centralia, Illinois. His father, Grover, was a railroad hostler, servicing trains at the railyard. His mother, Mabel, was a homemaker, raising David and his three younger siblings. Even before attending school, David showed great intelligence. He learned to read on his own before starting elementary school.

Though segregation was prominent across the country, David attended integrated schools. He was spared some of the racial challenges Black students experienced elsewhere. David proved to be an exceptional student. He skipped grades twice in elementary school. He also excelled in high school, graduating in 1935 when he was only sixteen.

After high school, he enrolled in the University of Illinois at Urbana-Champaign. He chose to study mathematics. Though he had a scholarship, David also worked various jobs to earn money. He did not want his family to have to pay for anything while he was in college. In 1938, David received a Bachelor of Arts in mathematics.

David decided he wanted to teach at a university, so he began graduate studies and earned his master's degree in 1939. In 1941, at the age of 22, David received his PhD. His **dissertation** was called "Properties of Markov Chains." A Markov chain is a way to predict a sequence of events. David would return to this field of statistics in his later work.

Early in his career, racism placed roadblocks in David's path to success. His mentor, Professor Joseph L. Doob, helped him secure the Rosenwald Fellowship at the Institute for Advanced Study (IAS). Previous Rosenwald fellows taught and worked at Princeton University. But Princeton objected to David's appointment because he was Black. He was not allowed to do research or even attend lectures there. Professor Doob and the IAS insisted

David be treated fairly. Princeton eventually agreed and allowed David to continue his work.

David's time at IAS started him on a journey that would lead to some of his most significant accomplishments. At IAS, David had the opportunity to work with John von Neumann. John is known as the father of modern game theory. Game theory studies how decisions are made in competitive situations. It is used to develop strategies in business, the military, and sports.

John sent David a note requesting a meeting to discuss David's paper on Markov chains. David thought John was too important to be interested in mentoring students, so he didn't think John was serious. David avoided the meeting, and it almost didn't happen. When they eventually met, however, David was impressed at John's willingness to mentor others. He inspired David to do the same. In his career, David mentored over 50 students as they prepared their doctoral dissertations.

Racism also affected David when he applied for a teaching job at a university. In 1942, David interviewed at the University of California, Berkeley. He was not offered the position. Years later, David discovered that he was not hired because he was Black. The department chair often hosted faculty members in his home, and his wife did not want a Black man in her house. As a result, the school refused to hire him.

David applied to work at over 100 Black colleges around the country. He accepted a position at Southern

University in Baton Rouge, Louisiana. A year later, he taught at Clark College. In 1944, Howard University offered David a position in its math department. He remained at Howard for 10 years. During that time, he became a full professor and head of the department.

While at Howard, David also worked for the RAND Corporation. RAND is a research organization that works with countries and corporations to make policy decisions. At RAND, David met Abe Girshick, a fellow statistician. His friendship with Abe led to David returning to game theory. Their collaboration resulted in a 1954 book called *Theory of Games and Statistical Decisions*. The book is considered a classic.

Also in 1954, David was invited to lecture at UC Berkeley. After his lecture, the university offered David the position he had interviewed for 12 years earlier. He accepted and became the head of the statistics department a year later. David stayed at UC Berkeley until his retirement in 1988.

In 2014, four years after his death, David was awarded the National Medal of Science. His work had a lasting impact on many fields, including drug testing, computer communications, and manufacturing. His mentoring had a lasting impact on generations of students that followed.

"[GEOMETRY] WAS THE ONLY COURSE I HAD THAT MADE ME SEE THAT MATHEMATICS IS REALLY BEAUTIFUL AND FULL OF IDEAS."

EXPLORE MORE! One of David's areas of focus was game theory. Learn more about it in *Introducing Game Theory: A Graphic Guide* by Ivan Pastine and Tuvana Pastine. It's illustrated by Tom Humberstone.

DID YOU KNOW? Modern game theory is said to have originated with John von Neumann and Oskar Morgenstern in 1944. Some of its principles, however, go back to ancient times. Even the Greek philosopher Socrates is credited with presenting ideas that fit within game theory.

Roy L. CLAY SR.

1929–present

Since the 1960s, the Northern California region of Silicon Valley has been home to technological innovation. There are many people who contributed to the growth and success of Silicon Valley. Roy L. Clay Sr. was one man who made an impact on its corporations and its community. As an engineer, Roy led the creation of one of the first minicomputers. He also started a company that became a leader in electronics testing. He brought hundreds of African Americans into the technology industry. Because of his influence, Roy is often called the Godfather of Silicon Valley.

Roy was born in Kinloch, Missouri, in 1929. His parents were Charles and Emma Clay. At that time, Kinloch was an all-Black community just outside Ferguson, Missouri. Roy grew up in a caring environment where everyone encouraged him to succeed.

As a young boy, Roy would walk to Ferguson to earn money doing gardening work. One day, on his way home, the police stopped him because he was in a white neighborhood. They handcuffed him, put him in a police car, and drove him to the Ferguson town limits. When they let him go, they warned him not to return to Ferguson. When Roy told his mother about his run-in with the police, she gave him advice that would change his life. "You will experience racism for the rest of your life, but don't ever let that be a reason why you don't succeed," she said. Roy always remembered his mother's words.

Roy attended Douglass High School. After graduation, he earned an academic scholarship to Saint Louis University. It was the first college in a former slave state to integrate. In 1946, Roy was one of the first African American students to attend the university. He graduated in 1951 and began looking for a job.

Roy applied for a position at McDonnell Aircraft after graduation. Because of his success in college, he was invited to interview with the company. McDonnell didn't realize that Roy was Black. When he arrived for his interview and they saw him in person, Roy was sent away. He was told the company did not hire "professional Negroes."

Remembering his mother's advice, Roy did not let the incident keep him from succeeding. He taught himself computer programming. In 1958, Roy got a job at what is now the Lawrence Livermore National Laboratory. There, he wrote his first software program. The program calculated how **radiation** would spread after a nuclear explosion. In 1962, Roy went to work for Control Data Corporation as a software engineer. At Control Data, he developed software to make computers easier to use.

Because of his previous work, Roy attracted the attention of Dave Packard. Dave was the cofounder of Hewlett-Packard (HP). At the time, HP was a new company focused on building **semiconductors**. In 1965, HP planned to launch a new computer division. Roy was invited to interview there. Though he wasn't interested at first, Roy agreed to the interview. After two days of interviews, he accepted the job. Roy became responsible for the development of HP's first minicomputer. The HP 2116A was the size of a typewriter, which was unique at that time. Most early computers were much, much larger. Some filled entire rooms.

Roy was the first director of HP's research and development computer group. Later, he became general manager of the computer division of Hewlett-Packard. Roy also worked as a consultant for Kleiner Perkins Caufield & Byers, an investment group that provided money to emerging businesses. He helped them identify technology companies that would make a good investment. He recommended investing in Tandem Computers, Compaq, and Intel. All three went on to revolutionize the computer industry and become billion-dollar companies.

In 1977, Roy founded ROD-L Electronics. The company designs and builds electronic test equipment for computers and other devices. Manufacturers use the equipment to prove their products are safe. The first testing device certified by Underwriters Laboratories was invented by Roy at ROD-L. Today, Roy still serves as the CEO of the company.

Roy also worked to give other African Americans opportunities. He served on the Palo Alto City Council from 1973 to 1979. He was the first person of color to serve on the council.

In the 1970s, President Richard Nixon proposed reducing services to African American communities. The policy was called "benign neglect." Roy was concerned about how this would affect Black workers trying to break into his industry. In response, he created new programs to help Black people seeking careers in the technology field.

Roy overcame bigotry to get an education and build a career for himself. Along the way, he helped shape the technology industry. His leadership came at a time when Silicon Valley was still new and unproven. Since then, it has become a world leader in innovation. Along the way, Roy made time to help other Black engineers. He felt that good character was just as important as education. He wouldn't let someone's lack of education prevent them from getting a job. If they could show that they had the interest and skill to succeed, he would hire them. Many African Americans have since made contributions in the world of technology thanks to the Godfather of Silicon Valley.

"MY FIRST TEACHER INSPIRED ME TO DO WELL. BY THE TIME I LEFT THAT LITTLE SCHOOL, I THOUGHT I COULD LEARN TO DO ANYTHING."

EXPLORE MORE! Check out the Tech Interactive, a science and technology center located in San Jose, the heart of Silicon Valley. You can visit or take a virtual tour at TechforTomorrow.com/virtual-field-trip.

DID YOU KNOW? In 1988, Roy became the first African American member of the Olympic Club in San Francisco, California. The Olympic Club is the oldest athletic club in the United States. It has hosted five U.S. Open Golf Championships.

James Edward Maceo WEST

1931–present

Anyone who makes a phone call, wears a hearing aid, or plays with a talking doll uses technology made by James E. West. James overcame the hardships of racism and war to become one of the 20th century's most significant inventors. After a career that saw him obtain more than 200 patents, James went to work in academia, passing on his knowledge to the next generation of inventors.

James was born in Virginia on February 10, 1931. His father, Samuel, worked various jobs. He sold insurance, worked as a railroad porter, and ran a funeral home. James's mother, Matilda, was schoolteacher. Her employers did not approve of her involvement in the civil rights movement. As a result, she lost her job.

When he was young, James was fascinated by electronic equipment. At the age of 10, he found an old radio someone had thrown away and tried to plug it in. James electrocuted himself. The accident left him sore, but it also inspired him. By the time he was 12, James was working alongside his cousin, installing electrical wiring in homes in his community.

James graduated from Phoenix High School and enrolled at Hampton University in Virginia. Because of racism in the South, his parents were concerned about James's career opportunities. His father believed that Black people should focus on the jobs most open for them: teacher, doctor, lawyer, or preacher. James chose to study to be a doctor. His education was interrupted by the start of the Korean War. James was drafted into the United States military and served overseas. He was awarded the Purple Heart, an honor given to soldiers who are injured or killed in combat.

After the war, James returned to his studies and transferred to Temple University. He also changed his field of study from medicine to physics. James's decision made his parents unhappy. They stopped helping him pay for school, but James still stuck with his decision.

During the summers, James worked as an intern at Bell Laboratories. The company was founded in 1925 to ensure that Alexander Graham Bell's telephone system was successfully installed across the country. It became a leader in innovation for the next century. James was assigned to Bell's **acoustic** research department. When he graduated from Temple University in 1957, James went to work as a scientist at Bell Laboratories full time. He was one of very few Black scientists at Bell.

During his time at Bell, James collaborated with fellow engineer Gerhard M. Sessler. In 1960, they created a small, inexpensive microphone that picked up very low sounds. Their first version of this microphone required a 500-volt battery. The battery was bigger than a refrigerator! It also only worked for a short time before fizzling out. So, they kept experimenting. James soon discovered that he could charge the microphone for a long period of time by reversing the **polarity** of the battery. After that, the microphone no longer needed the battery.

The invention became known as the **electret** microphone. Electrets are materials that can maintain an electric charge over a long period of time. Because it didn't require a battery, the electret microphone could be as small as a shirt button. After a few more adjustments, Gerhard and James's invention was complete.

In 1968, the electret microphone was being mass-produced. The microphones were used for telephones but were also game changers for people who used hearing aids. Previously, hearing aids were bulky and required large batteries. They also produced a constant vibration, which made them uncomfortable to wear for long periods of time. With electret microphones, hearing aids were smaller and much more comfortable. They could be worn all the time without causing discomfort. Today, 90 percent of microphones are based on the electret microphone. This includes those in cell phones, toys, hearing aids, and other medical devices.

James continued innovating at Bell Laboratories for four decades. He enjoyed the chance to collaborate with scientists in many different disciplines. For example, he worked with NASA to create health-monitoring equipment that could be used in space. He also helped develop sensors to detect toxic chemicals to save lives around the world.

In 2001, James retired from Bell Laboratories. He still wanted to work, so he took a position at Johns Hopkins University in Baltimore, Maryland. The environment of openness and innovation at Johns Hopkins reminded him of Bell Labs. He fit right in.

In addition to his scientific research, James is known for his dedication to mentoring students. He continues to give his time to organizations that encourage women and people of color to pursue careers in science and technology.

Throughout his career, James worked to create and innovate because he loved science. He published more than 150 papers and was awarded over 200 US and international patents. In 1999, he was inducted into the National Inventors Hall of Fame. In 2006, President George W. Bush presented James with the National Medal of Technology and Innovation.

Surprisingly, James only earned one dollar for each of the patents he was awarded while working at Bell Laboratories. This was Bell's standard practice, and it never bothered James. He didn't care about the money. He just enjoyed doing something he loved.

"A SCREWDRIVER AND PLIERS WERE VERY DANGEROUS. ANYTHING THAT HAD SCREWS IN IT, I COULD OPEN UP."

EXPLORE MORE! Want to learn more about the inventors and inventions that have changed our world? Take a virtual tour of the National Inventors Hall of Fame at ArtsandCulture.Google.com/partner/national-inventors-hall-of-fame-museum.

DID YOU KNOW? In 2018, James was awarded the John Scott Medal in recognition of his contribution to the "comfort, welfare and happiness" of humankind.

Frank S. GREENE JR.

1938–2009

Frank S. Greene Jr. was many things in his life. As a technologist, he helped design the fastest computer memory chips ever produced. As an entrepreneur, he founded two successful companies. As a venture capitalist, he funded numerous startups run by minorities and women. As a mentor, he helped guide young people into careers in technology. Frank's many successes all came down to one thing: being prepared to succeed. It was a lesson he learned early in life.

Frank was born on October 19, 1938, in Washington, DC. His father, Frank Sr., and his mother, Olivia, both worked for the government. Frank began attending elementary school in Washington, DC. When his father was transferred, the family moved to St. Louis, Missouri. There, Frank attended Cole School. He enjoyed math and science classes and did well in them.

After elementary school, Frank attended Sumner High School. Sumner was the first high school for African

Americans west of the Mississippi River. During his senior year at Sumner, Frank decided to pursue a career in engineering. He didn't know any engineers, but he knew he enjoyed math and physics. Engineering seemed like a perfect fit.

After being offered a scholarship to Washington University, Frank decided to enroll there. Washington had recently allowed Black students to attend, and Frank was in the second integrated class. Still, there were fewer than 10 Black students out of the 3,000 on campus. This left Frank and the other students of color feeling a little out of place.

Frank focused on his studies, but something else was calling him to action. Across the country, Black students were staging sit-ins. These protests against segregation took place in restaurants and other public places. Frank and his friends decided to stage sit-ins in their community. They would go to a restaurant, sit down, and wait to be served. In most cases, the staff would ignore them. Sometimes, they would call the police. But Frank and his friends persisted.

One day, they went to a pizza parlor in town. They sat down at a table expecting to be ignored. The staff came over to the table. They handed out menus and brought glasses of water for Frank and his friends. That's when Frank discovered that none of them had money to buy anything. That day, Frank realized that you must always be prepared for success. You don't want to succeed and not be ready.

While he was at Washington University, Frank served as a cadet in the Air Force Reserve Officer Training Corps. He was admitted to the Distinguished Military Cadet program. This meant that the Air Force would pay to send him to graduate school. So, when Frank graduated from Washington University in 1961, his next stop was Purdue University. He earned his Master of Science in electrical engineering from Purdue in 1962. After that, he served four years on active duty in the Air Force. He spent most of that time assigned to the National Security Agency in Fort Meade, Maryland.

When he left the Air Force in the mid-1960s, Frank had to find a new job. After he sent his résumé to several companies, Fairchild Semiconductor offered him a position in its research and development labs. Frank moved all the way across the country to take the job in California.

At Fairchild, Frank led a team that developed memory chips for high-speed computers. The memory chips, which stored information, were the fastest and largest chips at the time. His team was awarded a patent for its work.

At that same time, Frank enrolled in a part-time graduate program at Santa Clara University. In 1970, he earned his PhD in electrical engineering. A year later, Frank decided it was time to do something different. He left Fairchild and founded two different companies over the next decade.

Frank's first company was Technology Development Corporation (TDC). TDC created software programs for the Air Force's F-16 fighter jet and for NASA's space shuttle program. The second company he founded was ZeroOne Systems. ZeroOne sold powerful computer systems to the government for use in engineering and research. After building both companies into successful ventures, Frank decided to invest in the growth and development of other companies. This was the start of New Vista Capital.

New Vista Capital was a venture capital firm. Venture capital firms invest money and resources in new businesses to help them grow. New Vista focused on helping businesses started by women and minorities.

Frank was a technologist whose contributions earned him a place in the Silicon Valley Hall of Fame. He overcame segregation and discrimination to find success in an industry where Black people were rarely participants. How did he do it? He believed in himself, worked hard, and prepared for success. Along the way, Frank made time to help others. He taught at universities like Howard, Stanford, and Santa Clara. He mentored young people and even lent his name to the Dr. Frank S. Greene Jr. Scholars Program. The program provides resources for African American students to succeed in science and math.

Frank was once asked how he'd like to be remembered. His answer? "He did the best he could while he was here."

"YOU HAVE TO BE PREPARED FOR OPPORTUNITY WHEN IT ARRIVES. YOU'VE GOT TO BE PREPARED FOR SUCCESS."

EXPLORE MORE! Here's a chance to learn more about science and technology from the comfort of your home. Check out the Pacific Science Center's Curiosity at Home at PacificScienceCenter.org/events-programs/curiosity-at-home.

DID YOU KNOW? In recognition of his service to humanity, Frank was knighted in 2002. He was admitted as a Knight of Honor to the Sovereign Order of St. John of Jerusalem, Knights Hospitaller.

Guion Stewart BLUFORD JR.

1942–present

Growing up, Guion "Guy" Bluford Jr. believed he could and should follow his dreams. His love of airplanes took him to the United States Air Force, where he flew combat missions in a state-of-the-art fighter jet. He pursued graduate degrees in **aerospace** engineering and was selected to become a NASA astronaut. Guy became the first African American in space. His accomplishments inspired many to follow in his footsteps.

Guy was born in Philadelphia, Pennsylvania, on November 22, 1942. His mother, Lolita, was a teacher. His father, Guion Bluford Sr., was a mechanical engineer. Guy's parents and grandparents were college educated. His family expected him to get an education. They also encouraged him to work hard to reach his goals. As a result, Guy believed he could accomplish anything.

As a boy, Guy was interested in math and science. He enjoyed building model airplanes. By the time he reached high school, he planned to become an aerospace engineer.

He graduated from Overbrook High School in 1960. Then he enrolled at Pennsylvania State University.

At Penn State, Guy majored in aerospace engineering. He also joined the Air Force Reserve Officer Training Corps (ROTC). ROTC is a college program that trains students for careers in the military. Guy graduated from Penn State in 1964 with a Bachelor of Science in aerospace engineering. He was also **commissioned** as a second lieutenant in the United States Air Force.

That year, Guy enrolled in the Air Force's pilot training program at Williams Air Force Base. He received his pilot's wings in 1966. He then continued in the combat training program, where he learned to fly the F-4C Phantom. The F-4C was the Air Force's newest fighter plane.

After combat training, Guy transferred to the 557th Tactical Fighter Squadron in Vietnam. He flew 144 combat missions, including more than 50 over North Vietnam. In 1967, Guy returned to the United States. He became a flight instructor at Sheppard Air Force Base in Texas. For five years, he passed on his knowledge to new classes of Air Force pilots.

As his career progressed, Guy continued his education. In 1972, he entered the Air Force Institute of Technology Residency School. In 1974, he earned a Master of Science degree in aerospace engineering. Four years later, he earned his PhD in the same discipline.

While working on his dissertation, Guy received news that changed his life. He had been selected for NASA's eighth class of astronaut candidates. He was one of 35 selected out of more than 8,000 applicants.

A year later, in August 1979, Guy officially became a NASA astronaut.

For four years, Guy performed technical assignments supporting the early space shuttle missions. Then, on August 30, 1983, Guy climbed aboard the space shuttle *Challenger*. As *Challenger* blasted off, Guy became the first African American to fly in space.

After a successful first mission, Guy flew three more times in space. In 1985, he flew on board the last successful mission of *Challenger*. During the flight, he led 76 experiments in space. Guy's third flight launched in 1991. During the flight, Guy helped launch five satellites. Then, in 1992, Guy made his final trip to space with the space shuttle *Discovery*. On this mission, he conducted classified experiments that could only be performed by military personnel.

When Guy returned to Earth for the final time, he had flown four missions and logged 688 hours in space. He retired from the Air Force in 1993 with the rank of colonel. He also retired from NASA that same year.

Guy received many accolades and awards during his history-making career. In the Air Force, he earned the Distinguished Flying Cross, the Defense Superior Service Medal, and the Defense Meritorious Service Medal. As an astronaut, he received the NASA Outstanding Leadership Medal and was awarded the NASA Exceptional Service Medal three times. Guy's greatest contribution, however, may be the inspiration he sparked in the hearts and minds of millions of Americans when he soared into space and into history.

"I WANTED TO SET THE STANDARD, DO THE BEST JOB POSSIBLE SO THAT OTHER PEOPLE WOULD BE COMFORTABLE WITH AFRICAN AMERICANS FLYING IN SPACE AND AFRICAN AMERICANS WOULD BE PROUD OF BEING PARTICIPANTS IN THE SPACE PROGRAM."

EXPLORE MORE! Learn more about Guy's historic NASA career in the NASA virtual gallery at NASA.gov/subject/11054/guy-bluford.

DID YOU KNOW? Guy was one of three African American astronauts in his class. Fred Gregory and Ronald McNair were the other two. In 1986, Ronald McNair and the rest of the crew were lost when *Challenger* broke apart just after launch. This was one year after Guy's final flight on board *Challenger.*

Keith L. BLACK

1957–present

Keith L. Black was born in the heart of the segregated South. Despite the challenges this presented, he followed his passion for science and became a world-renowned **neurosurgeon**. Throughout his career, his skill with a scalpel and his medical discoveries helped countless patients. His innovations have changed the field of neurosurgery forever.

Keith was born in Tuskegee, Alabama, on September 13, 1957. His father, Robert, was an elementary school principal. His mother, Lillian, was a teacher. Even though the Supreme Court had said segregation was unconstitutional, it was still the law in Alabama. This meant that educational options for Black students were still very limited. Nonetheless, Keith found ways to learn and grow. He loved science and taught himself to dissect frogs. His father even bought him a cow's heart to dissect.

By the time he was 10, Keith's family moved north to Ohio. They settled in Cleveland, where Keith's father felt his sons would have better opportunities than they did in Alabama. He was right. In eighth grade, Keith would ride his bicycle to Case Western Reserve University. There, he would sit in the medical school library and search through *Index Medicus* for interesting science topics. *Index Medicus* was a publication that provided brief descriptions of scientific articles.

At Case Western, Keith met an oncologist, someone who studies and treats cancer. Impressed by Keith's interest in science, the oncologist told him about a research apprenticeship program. Keith was admitted to the program and began to learn basic laboratory skills. Keith's experiences increased his interest in science and medicine.

In high school, Keith got a job at St. Luke's Hospital in Cleveland. He assisted Frederick Cross and Richard Jones, who had invented the Cross-Jones artificial heart valve. The valve was used to help patients whose hearts weren't working properly. Working at St. Luke's, Keith performed surgeries on dogs, including transplants and heart valve replacements.

Keith began to wonder about the effects of the heart valves on blood cells. He convinced Frederick to allow him to use the lab's electron microscope to conduct research. At age 17, he collected his findings in his first paper. The paper won him honors status in the Westinghouse Science Talent Search in 1975.

After graduating from high school, Keith enrolled in the University of Michigan. He was admitted to its medical school's accelerated program. This allowed him to complete his undergraduate degree and his medical degree in only six years. Typically, it would take a student eight years or more to earn both degrees.

Keith discovered that he could handle the accelerated courses, so he turned his attention back to research. After his first class in neuroanatomy, the study of the brain, Keith wanted to focus on the brain. His early research was aimed at stroke prevention. This led him to more detailed scientific studies of the brain.

In 1981, at the age of 23, Keith received his medical degree. He completed his internship and his residency at the University of Michigan. In 1987, he moved to California to work at the University of California, Los Angeles. There, he became an assistant professor of neurosurgery and specialized in treating brain tumors.

Neurosurgeons face challenges removing tumors from the brain. It can be difficult to remove the tumor without damaging the brain. For the next 10 years, Keith worked to improve the methods used to treat brain tumors. He developed new techniques for removing them and also created new methods for treating them without surgery. Because of his efforts, Keith's reputation as a neurosurgeon grew.

In 1997, Keith accepted a position at Cedars-Sinai Medical Center in Los Angeles. At Cedars-Sinai, Keith developed a new method for treating brain tumors. This method used the body's natural immune system to fight the tumor. Keith's research showed very promising results almost immediately.

Keith continues to perform brain surgeries. He performs two to three times the number of surgeries as other neurosurgeons. He has even found ways to remove tumors other doctors believed were **inoperable**. In the first 20 years of his career, Keith performed more than 5,000 surgeries.

In 2007, Keith opened the Johnnie L. Cochran Jr. Brain Tumor Center in Los Angeles. The Cochran Center is named after Keith's longtime friend and patient, attorney Johnnie Cochran. There, Keith continues his research in hopes of finding more lifesaving discoveries.

Keith also helped start a program called Brainworks, which gives seventh and eighth graders a chance to learn about neuroscience. He volunteers his time with other similar programs around the United States.

From his humble beginnings, Keith followed his passion. It led him to a career in medicine. It also made him one of the world's most respected surgeons. His curiosity, skill, and hard work shaped him into a doctor with the power to change lives—and save them.

"I THINK [SUCCESS IS] A COMBINATION OF LUCK, DISCIPLINE, THE RIGHT NURTURING, AND THE RIGHT ENVIRONMENT."

EXPLORE MORE! Want to learn more about the brain and how it works? Check out Neuroscience for Kids! at Faculty.Washington.edu/chuler/neurok.html.

DID YOU KNOW? Keith doesn't spend all his time working. He loves the ocean and enjoys sailing and scuba diving. They are his way of relaxing from his very challenging job.

Rick KITTLES

1976–present

Many people take great pride in their heritage. Tracing their family's roots back for many generations gives people a sense of family and a connection with history. For many African Americans, though, this is difficult or impossible to do because of slavery. Africans were stolen from their homes and brought to America. Families were separated. They were often forbidden to speak their native languages. As a result, many African Americans have no idea where, exactly, they come from. This began to change in the late 20th century, thanks to the work of geneticist Rick Kittles.

Rick was born in Sylvania, Georgia, in 1976. When he was young, Rick moved to Central Islip, New York. In school, Rick was often the only Black student in his class. This made him start to wonder why everybody looked different. By the time he reached high school, Rick realized that his white classmates began to refer to themselves as Italian American or Irish American. He could only say his ancestors were from Africa when he was asked. It bothered him to not know where in Africa he was from.

After high school, Rick enrolled in the Rochester Institute of Technology in Rochester, New York. He chose to study science and graduated in 1989 with a degree in biology. Rick then enrolled in a graduate program at the College at Brockport. He continued studying biology, and before long, Rick realized that he wanted to become a research scientist. In order to do that, he would need to earn a PhD. Rick applied to George Washington University in Washington, DC, and was accepted.

While in graduate school, Rick's grandfather was diagnosed with prostate cancer. He passed away a short time later. Because of the experience of losing a family member, Rick chose prostate cancer research as one of his first fields of study.

In 1998, Rick earned his PhD from George Washington University and went to work at Howard University. He was an assistant professor of microbiology. He also became the director of the African American Hereditary Prostate Cancer Study Network at Howard's National Human Genome Center. The goal of this study was to determine whether there was a genetic marker that could explain why so many African American men were afflicted with prostate cancer. To do this, researchers looked for Black families with at least four family members with prostate cancer. They planned to take blood samples from the family members to study their DNA.

The project had difficulties almost from the start. One of the main issues was that the study was run by the government. Many African Americans were wary of participating because the government had previously used African American people as test subjects without their knowledge. The Tuskegee Study of Untreated Syphilis in the Negro Male in 1932 is one example. At Tuskegee Institute, the government told African American men with syphilis that they would be treated for "bad blood." Instead, the government only pretended to treat the men. They did not tell the men what they were sick with. Many became very ill or died, even though a simple treatment was available. As a result of this example and many others, many African Americans were reluctant to participate in the prostate cancer study.

During this time, Rick worked on another project that would have a significant impact on his career. The African Burial Ground Project was led by **anthropologist** Michael Blakey, who also worked at Howard University. The project studied the remains of over 400 African Americans who had been buried in a graveyard in New York City in the 1700s. Most of the research followed the normal anthropological methods. The caskets and clothes were studied to see if there were any links to African culture. The bones were studied for signs of how the people lived. Rick extracted DNA from the remains. He compared this DNA to DNA obtained from living Africans. Rick wanted to see if he could determine from where in Africa the people originated. This gave him an idea. If he could do this with remains that were two centuries old, could he do it for the living?

The answer was yes. Soon, Rick and his colleagues launched an ancestry project in Boston, Massachusetts. When word of the project got out, Rick received a lot of attention. Not all of it was good. Many people questioned whether he could accurately trace people's DNA. Others complained about Rick charging for the service. The negative publicity delayed the launch of Rick's new company, but he didn't give up. In 2003, African Ancestry, Inc. opened for business.

Before long, many African Americans signed up to use the service. Oprah Winfrey and Quincy Jones are among the tens of thousands who have traced their African roots using Rick's service.

Rick performs research today as a professor at City of Hope, a cancer center in Southern California. He also continues his work with African Ancestry. With both jobs, he brings hope and happiness to those he serves.

"I KNOW A LOT OF PEOPLE QUIT BECAUSE THEY EXPERIENCE FAILURE. YOU HAVE TO BE PERSISTENT."

EXPLORE MORE! Want to learn more about genetics? Check out the Gene Scene, provided by the American Museum of Natural History at AMNH.org/explore/ology/genetics.

DID YOU KNOW? The portion of our DNA that determines what individual people look like is only 0.1 percent. The rest of it is the same. This is proof that we're really not that different after all.

Glossary

abolitionist: a person who supported and worked for an end to slavery

acoustic: relating to sound and hearing

aerospace: the study and practice of flight, both within the Earth's atmosphere and in space

alma mater: a Latin phrase that describes the school or university someone attended

anthropologist: one who studies humankind, including cultures, migrations, and origins

biology: the study of all living things, including their anatomy, behavior, and origin

botany: the study of plants, including their physical structure, genetic makeup, and classification

census: an official count of people of living in a particular country or area

charter: to rent a commercial plane, boat, or other vehicle for private use

chemistry: the study of the substances that make up matter, including how they interact and combine

collaborate: work together with others to achieve a common goal or purpose

commission: grant an officer's rank to someone in the armed forces

dissertation: a research project completed as a requirement for a degree

electret: a piece of material that, when exposed to energy, becomes charged for a long period of time

emancipation: the process of setting individuals free from restrictions of a legal or social nature

engineering: the study and practice of designing and building structures (like buildings and bridges) and machines (like robots or engines)

incandescent: something that, when heated, gives off light

inoperable: unable to be operated on

intellectual property: an invention or creation that is unique and to which someone has the rights

microbiology: the study of living things that are too small to see with the human eye, like bacteria and viruses

neurosurgeon: a doctor whose specialty is performing procedures on the brain and spinal cord

patent: a license granting the holder rights to a creation or invention, which prevents others from making a creation of a similar design

pathology: the study of the cause and results of disease

philanthropist: a person who uses their time, talent, or money to help others who are in need

physics: the study of the nature and properties of energy and matter

polarity: the direction of the electric or magnetic charge of an item like a battery or magnet

porter: a person responsible for carrying packages, supplies, and luggage

prestigious: worthy of praise or admiration

probationary: a period during which a student or employee must prove themselves by meeting certain criteria

radiation: subatomic particles or electromagnetic waves caused by the release of energy

rehabilitation: a process that uses medicine and/or therapy to return someone to health

residency: advanced training in a medical profession, which usually follows graduation from medical school

segregated: divided by race, gender, or other social definitions

semiconductor: a material that is neither completely an insulator nor completely a conductor of electricity that is used in building electronic circuits

statistics: the science of using numerical data to make conclusions and predictions

surplus: an amount of material or money that remains after what is needed is used

synthetic: a substance made using chemical processes with the intent to simulate a compound that occurs in nature

tariff: a tax that must be paid when a particular product is imported or exported

tissue: organic substance found in plants and animals, including humans

valedictorian: a student with the highest achievement in his or her graduating class

zoology: the study of animals, including their physical structure, genetic makeup, and classification

Selected References

Abramson, C. I. "Charles Henry Turner: Contributions of a Forgotten African-American to Honey Bee Research." *American Bee Journal*. 2003. Psychology .Okstate.edu/museum/turner/turnerbio.html.

Academy of Achievement. "Keith L. Black." Accessed August 7, 2021. Achievement.org/achiever/keith -l-black.

Anderson, Brian. "Innovator's Spotlight: Col. Guion S. Bluford." Air Force News Services. April 16, 2021. AF.mil/News/Article-Display/Article/2575707 /innovators-spotlight-col-guion-s-bluford.

APS News. "June 1876: Edward Bouchet Becomes the First African American PhD in Physics." June 2007. APS.org/publications/apsnews/200706/history .cfm.

Boyd, Herb. "Dr. Harold Amos, the First Black Microbiologist." *New York Amsterdam News*. April 2, 2020. AmsterdamNews.com/news/2020/apr/02/dr -harold-amos-first-black-microbiologist.

Brief Biographies. "Rick Kittles–Directed Prostate Cancer Study." Accessed August 7, 2021. Biography .jrank.org/pages/2621/Kittles-Rick-Directed -Prostate-Cancer-Study.html.

Brillinger, David R., and J. W. Addison. "In Memoriam: David Harold Blackwell." Accessed July 29, 2021. Senate.UniversityOfCalifornia.edu/_files/inmemoriam/html/davidharoldblackwell.html.

Cavanaugh Simpson, Joanne. "Sound Reasoning." *Johns Hopkins Magazine.* September 2003. Pages.JH.edu/jhumag/0903web/west.html.

DNLee. "Charles Henry Turner, Animal Behavior Scientist." *Scientific American.* February 13, 2012. Blogs.ScientificAmerican.com/urban-scientist/charles-henry-turner-animal-behavior-scientist.

Dremann, Sue, and Chris Kenrick. "Frank Greene, Silicon Valley Technology Pioneer, Dies at 71." *Palo Alto Online.* December 28, 2009. PaloAltoOnline.com/news/2009/12/28/frank-greene-silicon-valley-technology-pioneer-dies-at-71.

George, Luvenia. "Innovative Lives: Lewis Latimer (1848–1928): Renaissance Man." Accessed July 19, 2021. Invention.SI.edu/innovative-lives-lewis-latimer-1848-1928-renaissance-man.

George, Luvenia. "Lewis Latimer: Renaissance Man Educational Materials." Accessed July 19, 2021. Invention.SI.edu/sites/default/files/Lewis_Latimer_Educational_Materials_by_Luvenia_George.pdf.

Goodman, James. "Leader in Genetic Ancestry Movement to Visit RIT." *Democrat and Chronicle.* August 2,

2014. DemocratAndChronicle.com/story/news/2014/08/02/rick-kittles-african-ancestry-rit/13512571.

Harvard Gazette. "Harold Amos—Faculty of Medicine: Memorial Minute." Accessed July 29, 2021. News.Harvard.edu/gazette/story/2007/02/harold-amos.

Hickins, Michael. "From Ferguson to Silicon Valley: A Black Pioneer Gives Back." *Forbes*. February 19, 2015. Forbes.com/sites/oracle/2015/02/19/from-ferguson-to-silicon-valley-a-black-pioneer-gives-back/?sh=37d7ba3930a1.

HistoryMakers. "Frank S. Greene." Accessed August 7, 2021. TheHistoryMakers.org/biography/frank-greene-jr.

Lujan, Heidi L., and Stephen E. DiCarlo. "First African-American to Hold a Medical Degree: Brief History of James McCune Smith, Abolitionist, Educator, and Physician." *Advances in Physiology Education*. April 1, 2019. Journals.Physiology.org/doi/full/10.1152/advan.00119.2018.

Morgan, Thomas M. "The Education and Medical Practice of Dr. James McCune Smith (1813–1865), First Black American to Hold a Medical Degree." *Journal of the National Medical Association*. July 2003. Accessed July 19, 2021. Ncbi.nlm.nih.gov/pmc/articles/PMC2594637.

NASA. "Guy Bluford Remembered 30 Years Later." Accessed August 7, 2021. NASA.gov/vision/space/workinginspace/bluford_1st_african_amer.html.

Odesanya, Nosayaba. "James West, Co-Inventor of the Modern Day Microphone." *New York Amsterdam News*. June 22, 2017. AmsterdamNews.com/news/2017/jun/22/james-west-co-inventor-modern-day-microphone.

Orphanides, Nicole. "Inventor and Mentor: Dr. Leonidas H. Berry and the Gastroscope." *Circulating Now: From the Historical Collections of the National Library of Medicine*. Accessed July 29, 2021. CirculatingNow.nlm.nih.gov/2018/07/19/inventor-mentor-dr-leonidas-h-berry-and-the-gastroscope.

Piana, Ronald. "A Pioneering Neurosurgeon Shares Hard-Earned Wisdom Gained along the Road from the Segregated South." *ASCO Post*. August 10, 2020. ASCOPost.com/issues/august-10-2020/a-pioneering-neurosurgeon-shares-hard-earned-wisdom-gained-along-the-road-from-the-segregated-south.

ROD-L Electronics, Inc. "Management—Roy Clay, Sr." Accessed July 29, 2021. RODL.com/management.html.

Science History Institute. "George Washington Carver." Accessed July 19, 2021. ScienceHistory.org/historical-profile/george-washington-carver.

About the Author

Bryan Patrick Avery was born and raised in Silicon Valley. He has worked in information technology for more than 25 years, holding leadership positions in several IT companies. Currently, Bryan is a chief technologist and systems development director for Peraton. He is also an award-winning poet and author of books for children, including *The Freeman Field Photograph* and the series Mr. Grizley's Class. Bryan lives in Northern California with his family.

About the Illustrator

Nikita Leanne is a London-based illustrator with a passion for comics, picture books, and storytelling. From lovable characters to beautiful backgrounds, she loves to create illustrations for stories that people can relate to, find comfort in, or be educated by. Some of the stories Nikita has told have centered around connecting with family and friends and educating young viewers on cultures they may never have heard of before—with the help of an adorable snake taking them through the story.